Video Games
From Then to Now

George Ivanoff

Video Games: From Then to Now

Text: George Ivanoff
Publishers: Tania Mazzeo and Eliza Webb
Series consultant: Amanda Sutera
Hands on Heads Consulting
Editor: Gemma Smith
Project editors: Annabel Smith and Jarrah Moore
Designer: Leigh Ashforth
Project designer: Danielle Maccarone
Permissions researchers: Helen Mammides and Lumina Datamatics
Production controller: Renee Tome

Acknowledgements
We would like to thank the following for permission to reproduce copyright material:

Front cover: littlewolf1989/Adobe Stock; pp. 1, 26 (top): Krakenimages.com/Shutterstock.com; p. 3: Golden Shark/Adobe Stock; p. 4: littlewolf1989/Adobe Stock; p. 5: Westend61 GmbH/Alamy Stock Photo; pp. 6, 28: Bernard Hoffman/LIFE Magazine; p. 7 (left): MediaWiki, (right): Emily743/Dreamstime LLC; p. 8 (top): Courtesy of the Computer History Museum, (bottom, p. 28): Joi Ito/Spacewar running on PDP-1/Flickr; p. 9: Volker Steger/Science Photo Library; p. 10 (top): INTERFOTO/Alamy Stock Photo, (bottom): iStock.com/Marc Dufresne; p. 11 (top): Ralph H. Baer/National Museum of American History/Smithsonian, (bottom): EXSHOW/Wikimedia Commons; p. 12 (top): Wirestock, Inc./Alamy Stock Photo, (bottom): iStock.com/kali9; pp. 13, 28, back cover: Emily743/Dreamstime LLC; p. 14 (top left): David Greedy/Getty Images, (bottom left, p. 28): INTERFOTO/Alamy Stock Photo, (right): Maurice Savage/Alamy Stock Photo; p. 15 (top): npp/Alamy Stock Photo, (bottom, p. 29): Scottamus, Ken/Flickr; p. 16: Interfoto/Alamy Stock Photo; p. 17 (top): Chris Willson/Alamy Stock Photo, (bottom): Editorial/Alamy Stock Photo; p. 18 (top): iStock.com/Panchof, (bottom): Jeff Gilbert/Alamy Stock Photo; p. 19 (top): Jose Luis Pelaez Inc/Getty Images, (bottom, p. 29): Mouse in the House/Alamy Stock Photo; p. 20 (top): Joe Haupt/Wikimedia Commons, CC BY-SA 2.0, (middle, p. 28); Evan-Amos/Wikimedia Commons, (bottom right): Nintendo of America/Getty Images, (bottom left, p. 29): Russell Hart/Alamy Stock Photo; p. 21 (top): Juan Diego Oliva Plaza/Alamy Stock Photo, (bottom): Sovfoto/Universal Images Group/Shutterstock.com; p. 22 (top): Future Publishing/Getty Images, (bottom): © Cengage; p. 23 (top, p. 28): INTERFOTO/Alamy Stock Photo, (left): Svitlana Bezuhlova/Shutterstock.com; (bottom): Roberta Williams and Sierra; p. 24 (main): Panther Media/Alamy Stock Photo; clockwise from top right: Syda Productions/Adobe Stock, iStock.com/blackCAT, iStock.com/travelism, WESTOCK/Adobe Stock; p. 25 (all): Friedrich Stark/Alamy Stock Photo; p. 26 (bottom): Gorodenkoff/Shutterstock.com; p. 27 (top): Pressmaster/Shutterstock.com, (bottom): JoeyPhoto/Shutterstock.com; p. 28 (bottom left): Jens Wolf/dpa/picture-alliance/Newscom; p. 29 (bottom left): kseniyaomega/Adobe Stock, (bottom right): Westend61/Getty Images, (middle right): Alex/Adobe Stock; p. 30: Westend61 GmbH/Alamy Stock Photo; p. 32: iStock.com/filo.

Every effort has been made to trace and acknowledge copyright. However, if any infringement has occurred, the publishers tender their apologies and invite the copyright holders to contact them.

NovaStar

ISBN 978 0 17 033471 6

Cengage Learning Australia
Level 5, 80 Dorcas Street
Southbank VIC 3006 Australia
Phone: 1300 790 853
Email: aust.nelsonprimary@cengage.com

For learning solutions, visit **cengage.com.au**

Printed in China by 1010 Printing International Ltd
1 2 3 4 5 6 7 29 28 27 26 25

Nelson acknowledges the Traditional Owners and Custodians of the lands of all First Nations Peoples. We pay respect to Elders past and present, and extend that respect to all First Nations Peoples today.

Contents

So Many Games!	4
The First Video Games	6
Early Game Consoles	10
Arcade Games	12
Home Consoles	16
Handheld Games	20
Home Computer Games	22
Virtual and Augmented Reality	26
Timeline	28
The Next Level	30
Glossary	31
Index	32

So Many Games!

Games have always been a fun part of our lives. We play all sorts of games – board games like Monopoly; strategy games like chess; physical sports games like basketball; and, of course, video games.

A video game is any electronic game controlled by a computer program that includes moving pictures shown on a TV, computer monitor or other form of video display.

There are many different types of video games. There are also many different ways to play them. You can play them on a computer or on a phone or tablet. You can play on a handheld **console** or a larger home console. Or you can play on a machine in an **arcade**.

Lots of people enjoy playing video games at home.

Gaming is a *huge* industry, making more than $2 billion a year. And gaming isn't just for kids. About 36% of gamers are between the ages of 18 and 34 years, and 15% are older than 55.

Gamers by Age

24% under 18

36% ages 18–34

13% ages 35–44

12% ages 45–54

9% ages 55–64

6% age 65+

This chart shows the different ages of video game players in the USA in 2022.

People of all ages can enjoy playing video games.

Video games have been around for a long time – longer than you might think. And they have **evolved** over time. The **graphics** have improved significantly, as has the level of storytelling and how **interactive** they are.

The history of video games is full of fun, competition and even education!

The First Video Games

It all began in the 1950s, when scientists needed a simple way to show people what computers were capable of doing. Games were a great way to demonstrate how computers could **interact** with people.

The first interactive games that scientists created were computer **versions** of simple existing games, like board games. The well-known pen-and-paper game Noughts and Crosses was updated to be played with computer technology in 1950. A machine called Bertie the Brain was displayed at a technology exhibition in Canada. The game on the machine was controlled using a keyboard, and the noughts and crosses were displayed on a grid of lights. The use of lights rather than a video screen meant that it was not technically a video game. But it was only one step away.

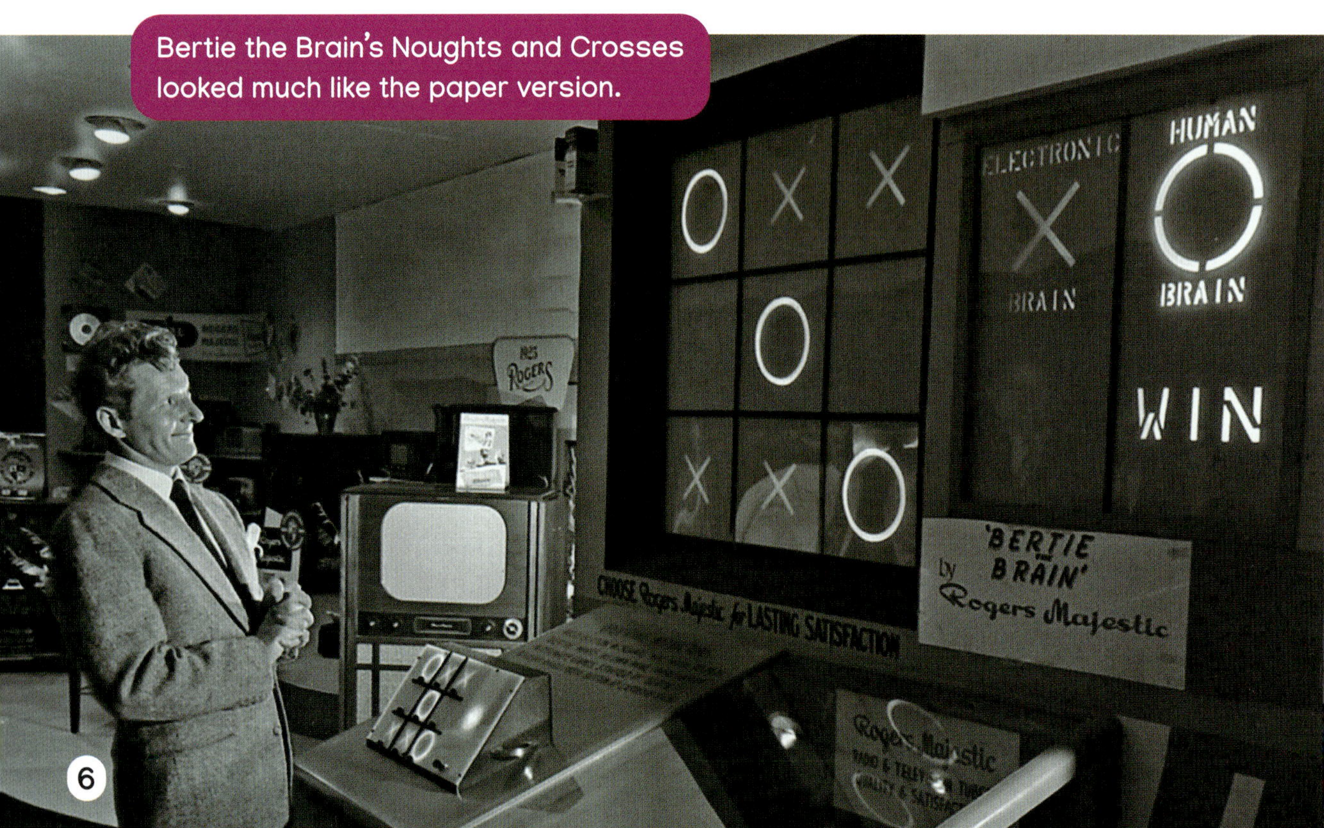

Bertie the Brain's Noughts and Crosses looked much like the paper version.

In 1952, British professor AS Douglas created a different version of Noughts and Crosses as part of his studies at the University of Cambridge in the United Kingdom. It was a **software** program that could be played on various computers. The noughts and crosses were displayed on a monochrome screen, meaning it only used one colour.

In 1958, scientist William Higinbotham created a tennis video game called *Tennis for Two*. Players used a special controller with a knob and a button to hit a "ball" over a line that represented a tennis net.

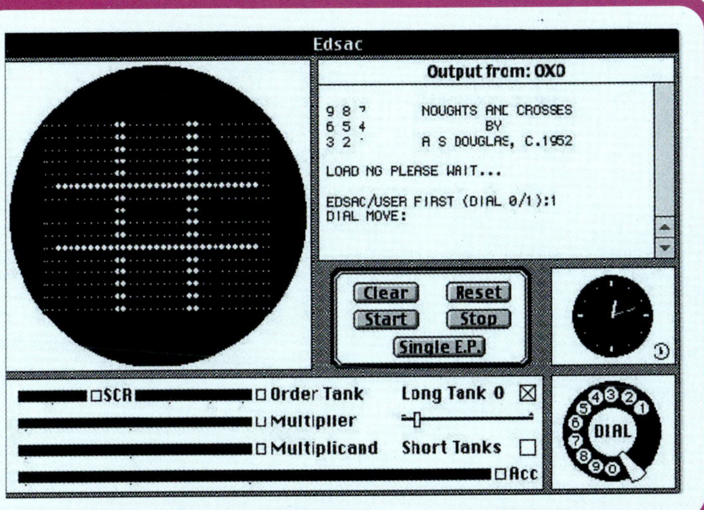

This simple game of Noughts and Crosses could be played on very early computers.

The images in *Tennis for Two* were simple green lines with a dot for the ball.

Hardware Versus Software

Bertie the Brain was a **hardware** version of Noughts and Crosses. It was a machine operated by a computer that was specifically designed and built to play one game only.

The software version of Noughts and Crosses used a computer program to play the game. It was played on computers that could also do other things.

In 1962, students and staff at the Massachusetts Institute of Technology in the USA created a game called *Spacewar*. The game was made to demonstrate what their new "minicomputer" could do. It was a space **combat** game in which players controlled two spaceships that battled against each other.

Two men play *Spacewar* together in the early 1960s.

Spacewar was soon made public and was given to anyone who asked for it ... for free! It was put on computers in other universities and became very popular with the students and staff. Before this, games were the property of those who created them, and could not be played anywhere other than at the university where they were created.

Spacewar could be played on a small computer.

As *Spacewar* was shared among universities and research centres, players changed it and added to it, creating new features.

This game would go on to inspire the first video games that the general public could buy and play.

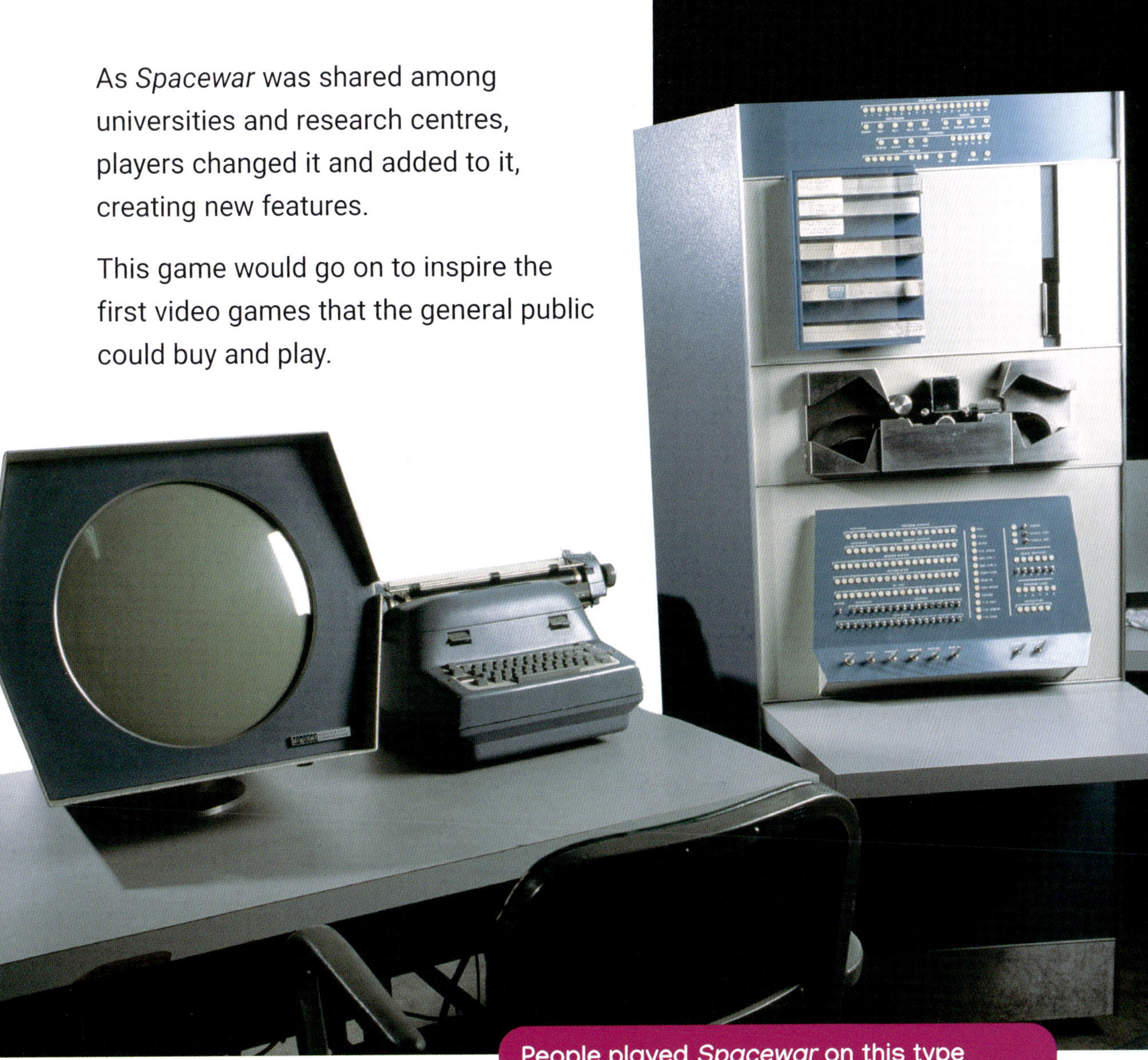

People played *Spacewar* on this type of computer, which was mostly used to control equipment in laboratories.

Retro Gaming

Old games are often recreated on modern game consoles and referred to as "retro games". Versions of *Spacewar* were recreated in 2012 and 2022 for modern consoles and computers.

Early Game Consoles

A game console is a device that can be connected to a TV and used to play video games. A console can be designed to play just one game, or it can play many games. It can be a single-player device that one person can use to play against the computer, or a multi-player device that two or more people can use to compete against each other.

A game console can be a great way to play video games with your family or friends.

A family plays a video game together in 1978.

Engineer Ralph Baer invented the first multi-player, multi-game console in 1967. It was known simply as the Brown Box. In 1972, an electronics company called Magnavox redesigned the Brown Box, changed its name to Odyssey and released it to the public.

The Brown Box got its name from its colour.

As an electronics company, Magnavox hoped that the Odyssey would help it sell more TVs. But its plan did not work. The Odyssey did not increase TV sales. In fact, the console did not sell well at all and was considered a failure.

The Brown Box was redesigned and called the Odyssey.

Black and White and Brown

Ralph Baer's console was called the Brown Box because the outside of it was covered in a brown wood-effect coating. The Odyssey was a white, black and brown box with two controllers connected to it by wires. The games were played on a TV and the graphics were all in black and white.

Arcade Games

An arcade game is any type of coin-operated machine that allows a player to play a particular game. These types of games include pinball machines, target games, fortune-telling machines and, of course, video games. They are usually found in arcades, but are also sometimes found in other places, such as bowling alleys and shopping centres.

The pinball machine is a popular arcade game.

There are still many places where you can play arcade games today.

The first arcade video game was created in 1971 by two American **electrical engineers**, Nolan Bushnell and Ted Dabney. Called *Computer Space*, it was inspired by *Spacewar*, which Bushnell had played when he was a student. *Computer Space* was a single-player game in which the player controlled a rocket and battled against two alien ships.

Around 1500 *Computer Space* machines were built and installed in arcades, universities and other places across the USA. The game was not successful. It was complicated and difficult to play, so people preferred playing traditional arcade games, like pinball. But Bushnell and Dabney did not give up.

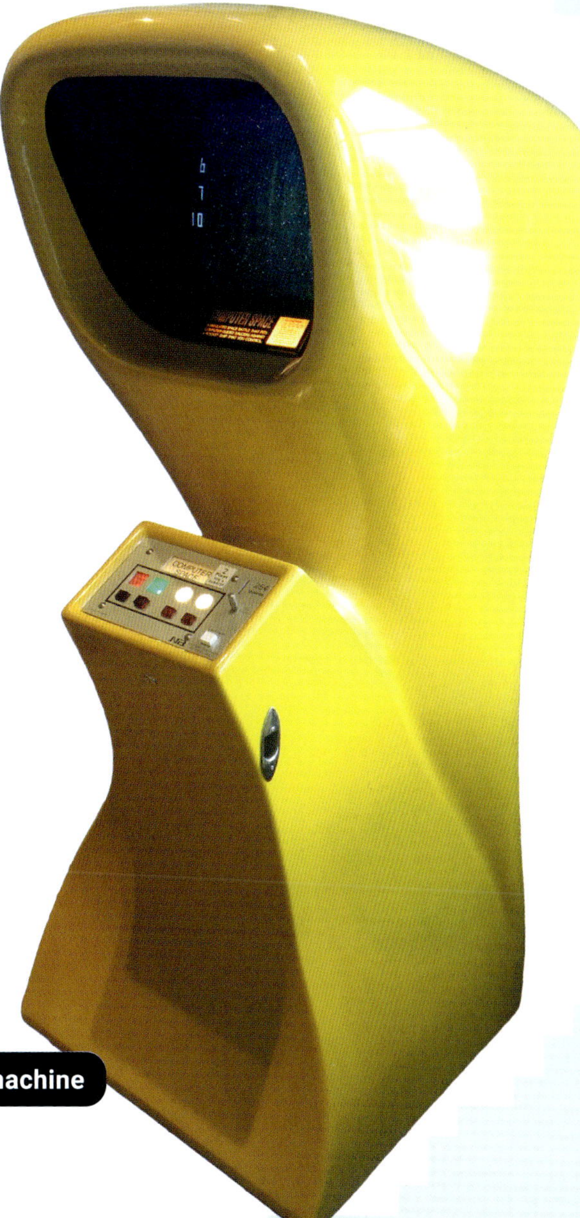

a ***Computer Space*** **machine**

Galaxy Game

At the same time that Bushnell and Dabney were creating *Computer Space*, two other electrical engineers were creating an arcade video game based on *Spacewar*. It was called *Galaxy Game*. *Computer Space* came out first and only two test versions of *Galaxy Game* were ever made.

In June 1972, Bushnell and Dabney formed a company called Atari and began work on their next arcade video game: *Pong*.

Pong was a simple version of table tennis, with a line down the middle of the screen representing the net, and a paddle (or bat) on either side. A "ball" bounced around the screen and players used a knob to control the up and down movement of their paddle as they tried to hit the ball.

Pong was released in November 1972 and was an immediate success! Unlike *Computer Space*, it was a very simple game that was easy to play. In fact, players could control it with one hand. The success of *Pong* led to more and more arcade games from various companies, including the famous game *Space Invaders* in 1978.

One player could even play both sides in *Pong*.

The short lines at either side are the "paddles" that players could move up and down in *Pong*.

Space Invaders was one of the first games to include background music.

Arcade video games are still popular today, and the sound and graphics continue to improve. Makers of these games are always looking to try new things to attract players. Some have been very successful, such as *Dance Dance Revolution*, released in 1998. Players dance on a special **platform** and match the dance moves as they appear on the video screen.

A boy plays *Dance Dance Revolution* in an arcade.

Other arcade games have not been so successful. The Japanese game *Cho Chabudai Gaeshi*, created in 2009, included a touch-sensitive tabletop attached to the front of the game machine. Players had to smack their hands onto the surface and then flip the tabletop over at the right time. Because the game was so unusual, it didn't gain massive success like *Dance Dance Revolution*.

Cho Chabudai Gaeshi

Competition

The first large-scale video game competition took place in 1980 in the USA. More than 10 000 people competed for the best score at *Space Invaders* in four tournaments held across the country, before a final in New York City. The final was won by woman called Rebecca Heineman.

Home Consoles

Inspired by the success of its *Pong* arcade video game, Atari created a version that people could play at home. In 1975, it released the *Home Pong* console, which could be connected to a TV. The console only played the one game in black and white. Like the arcade version, *Home Pong* was a huge success.

A mother and son play *Home Pong* together in 1976.

It was not long before other companies began making home consoles. Most of these were also single-game consoles. Some were just each company's own version of a table tennis game. But it was Atari again that achieved the next major success.

In 1977, Atari released the Atari 2600 home console. This console introduced three new things that would become standard in future consoles.

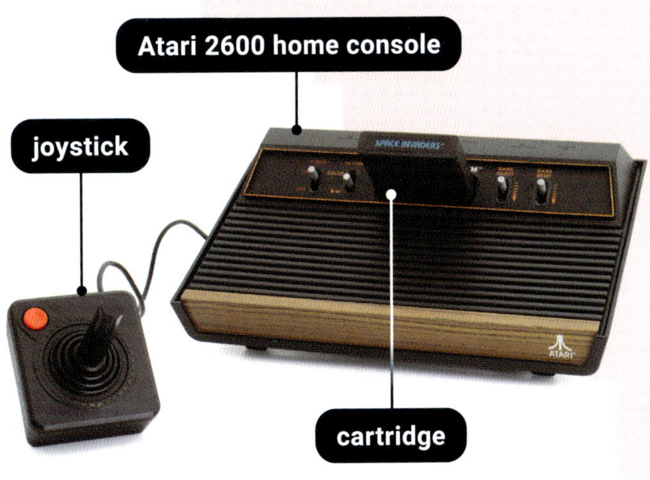

- a joystick, or lever that could be pushed and pulled to control movement in the game
- **interchangeable** cartridges (like small boxes) that each contained one game and could be swapped in and out
- colour graphics instead of black and white.

The bestselling game for the Atari 2600 was *Pac-Man*, released in 1982. It sold more than 7 million copies. The arcade version of *Pac-Man* was also very successful in the 1980s. *Pac-Man* has continued to be popular, with different versions being made for newer consoles. It is still enjoyed by many players today!

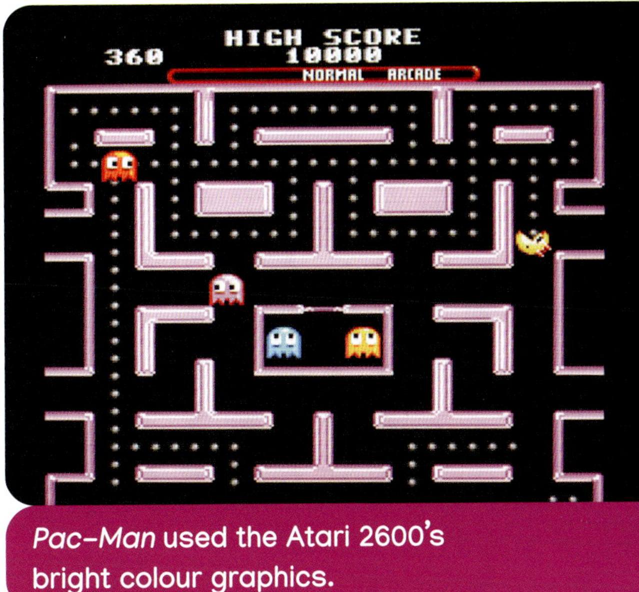

Pac-Man used the Atari 2600's bright colour graphics.

Pac-Man Ghost Names

Did you know that the ghosts in *Pac-Man* have names? They are called Clyde, Inky, Pinky and Blinky.

Home-console video games have continued to be popular, with new systems and features being introduced over the years.

game cartridges

Consoles switched from using games stored on cartridges to **CD-ROMs** in the early 1990s, to DVDs in the early 2000s and then to **Blu-ray** discs in the early 2010s. Today, games are often downloaded from the internet.

Another big development was **motion-sensitive** gaming. Some consoles, like the Nintendo Wii, were developed to work with motion-sensitive controllers. These controllers allowed players to play the game simply by moving the controller, rather than pressing buttons or operating a joystick. For example, a player could swing their controller like a racquet when playing a tennis game or move it around like a sword when playing a duelling game.

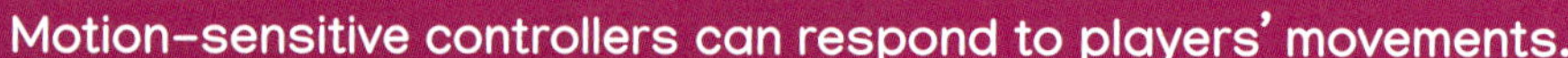

Motion-sensitive controllers can respond to players' movements.

Home consoles continue to evolve. Some modern consoles come with a camera that watches players and tracks their movements. This means that players can control a character in a game just by moving around.

Many consoles allow players to connect to the internet and play with people in different locations – from down the street to the other side of the world.

Always stay safe when playing online and only talk to people you know in real life.

Today, almost any kind of video game can be played on a home console.

Countless Consoles

More than a thousand different consoles have been released worldwide since home-console video games were introduced. According to a 2023 study, the highest-selling console of all time is Sony's PlayStation 2, with more than 155 million sold.

Handheld Games

Handheld video game consoles have a similar history to home consoles, in that they began with single-game devices. In fact, the first few handheld games were not really video games because they did not have images on a screen. They used tiny lights. *Auto Race* was the first of these games. Released in 1976, it used lights to represent racing cars.

***Auto Race* (1976)**

Handheld games with images on a screen were introduced in 1979. The first multi-game handheld console was called Microvision, and it could play a few simple games in black and white.

Although these early handheld consoles were popular, they did not sell as well as home consoles. It was not until the company Nintendo released the first Game Boy in 1989 that handheld games became really popular. In fact, the Game Boy is still the most successful gaming console ever made. It has had various different versions, each introducing updates including colour, improved graphics and better controls.

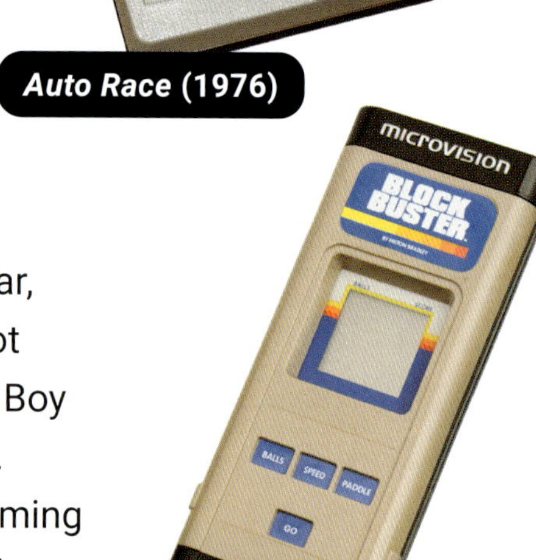

Microvision (1979)

original Game Boy (1989)

Game Boy Advance (2002)

Many handheld consoles have been released over the years and they are still popular today. Most current handheld consoles, like the Nintendo Switch, can connect to a TV as well. This means they can be used as a home console as well as a handheld console.

The controllers on the Nintendo Switch are motion-sensitive.

Game Boy in Space

In 1993, Russian **cosmonaut** Aleksandr A Serebrov took his Game Boy on a space mission. Later, it was bought at an auction for $1220.

Home Computer Games

Home computers became available in the 1970s. Although they were too expensive for most households when they were first released, by the end of the decade they had become more affordable.

Home computers were mostly used for work- and study-related activities such as **word processing**. But they were also used for playing games, as home-computer versions of arcade and console games became available.

Computer owners could also play text-based adventure games. These games used words rather than pictures to take the player on an adventure. It was a little bit like reading a book on a computer screen, except that the player typed instructions, solved puzzles and explored. The text described the surroundings and asked the player what they wanted to do. The player then typed a response such as "walk forward" or "open door".

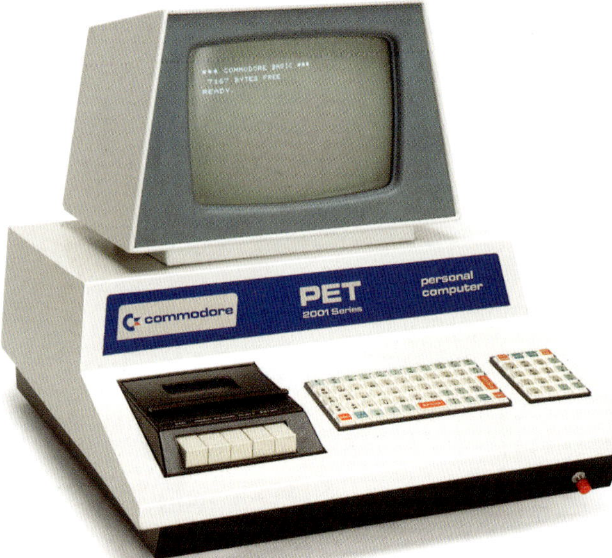

The Commodore PET was one of the first home computers.

We are in the hallway.

It is very dark but you can see
a door leading to the kitchen,
a door leading to the bathroom,
a cupboard,
and some stairs.

Where do you wish to go?

Kitchen

In text-based adventure games, the player typed what they wanted to do next.

The first popular text-based adventure game was *Zork* in 1977. It was a fantasy game in which the player explored the **ruins** of an underground city.

The first text-based adventure game to introduce images was *Mystery House* in 1980. The pictures were very simple computer illustrations using only straight lines.

Although text-based adventure games are not as popular today, many people still play them. In fact, these games are now also available on mobile devices, such as phones and tablets.

Zork was one of the earliest text-based adventure games.

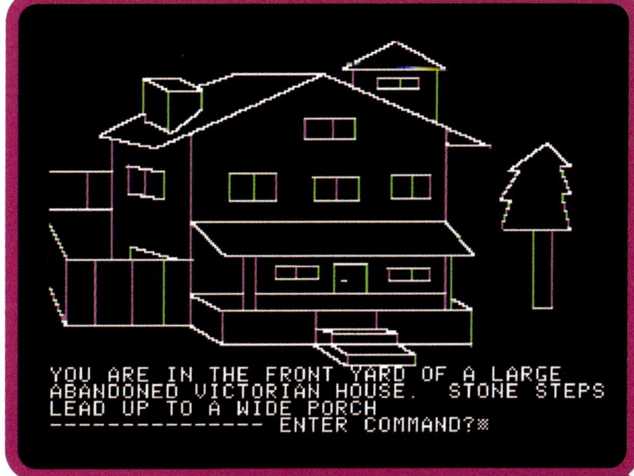

Mystery House included text and simple images.

Modern text-based adventure games can be played on a phone.

As more people bought home computers, online video games became increasingly popular. People could connect through the internet to play all sorts of games — from text-based adventures to more traditional video games. This was difficult at first, with slow and unstable internet connections. With the introduction of **broadband internet**, which was reliable and fast, online gaming increased. People were able to connect with other players around the world.

Broadband internet made connecting online faster and easier.

Multi-player, real-time, **virtual**-world games became popular with the release of *MUD1* (Multi User Dungeon) games in 1978. These were **role-playing games**, set in a virtual world that anyone could join. Players could explore the world, interact with other players, go on quests or engage in battles – all from the comfort of their homes. The early games were all text-based, but they eventually grew to include graphics.

Another Life?

Released in 2003, *Second Life* is a virtual-world game that **mimics** real life.

People create characters of themselves and play by getting their characters to do ordinary things, like shopping for clothes, getting a job or renting a house.

Virtual and Augmented Reality

Over the years, video game developers have tried to give players greater reality in their gaming experiences.

Virtual reality (VR) is a computer-generated 3D environment that players can interact with. The player wears goggles with inbuilt video screens that make it seem like the player is *in* the computer-generated world. They can interact with the VR world by using controllers or other devices, such as special gloves. Though originally developed for medical and scientific reasons (for example, to train doctors by allowing them to see inside a virtual human body), VR is now often used for video games.

A girl uses VR goggles to play a game.

With VR goggles, a player can feel as if they have entered a different world.

Augmented reality (AR) games put computer-generated images into the real world. The player holds a device with a camera and watches a screen that displays the real world, but computer-generated images also appear in the scene. Like VR, AR was developed for use in science, but is now also used for gaming.

AR games are common on handheld devices, such as phones and tablets. The best-known AR game is *Pokémon GO.*

Pokémon GO is an AR game that allows players to see video game creatures in the real world around them, using a phone or tablet.

Take Care!

When *Pokémon GO* was first released, people had accidents while walking or driving when they were playing the game. A study conducted in Tippecanoe County, USA, found that 134 car accidents between July and November in 2016 were caused by people playing *Pokémon GO* while driving.

Timeline

Technology and video games have come a very long way since Bertie the Brain in 1950. Have you played any of the games or used any of the consoles in this timeline?

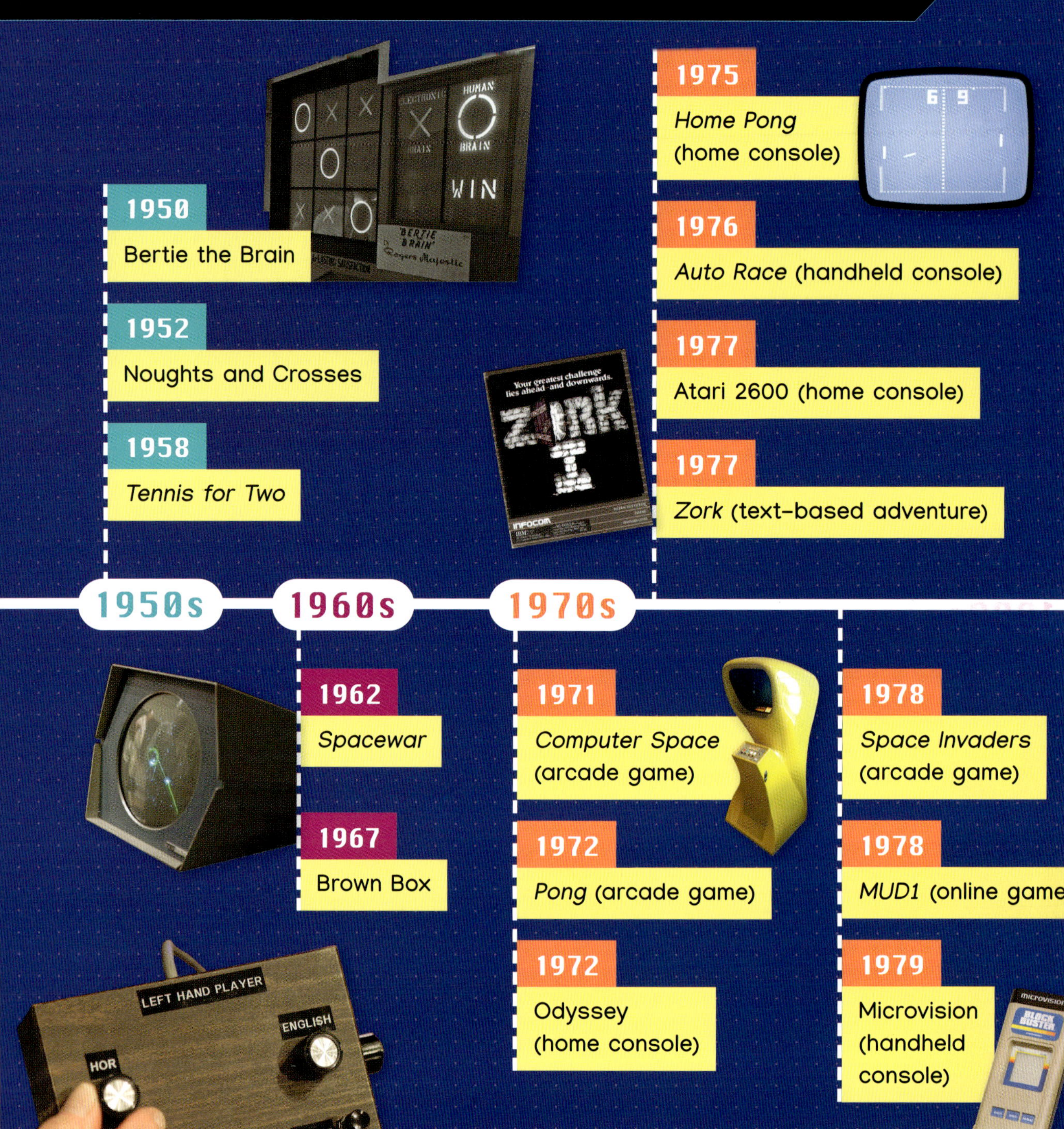

1950s

1950 Bertie the Brain

1952 Noughts and Crosses

1958 *Tennis for Two*

1960s

1962 *Spacewar*

1967 Brown Box

1970s

1971 *Computer Space* (arcade game)

1972 *Pong* (arcade game)

1972 Odyssey (home console)

1975 *Home Pong* (home console)

1976 *Auto Race* (handheld console)

1977 Atari 2600 (home console)

1977 *Zork* (text-based adventure)

1978 *Space Invaders* (arcade game)

1978 *MUD1* (online game)

1979 Microvision (handheld console)

1980
Mystery House (text-based adventure)

1989
Game Boy (handheld console)

1980s

1990s

early 90s
games on CD-ROM

1998
Dance Dance Revolution (arcade game)

2000s

2000
PlayStation 2

2003
Second Life (online game)

2009
Cho Chabudai Gaeshi (arcade game)

2016
Pokémon GO (AR game)

2017
Nintendo Switch (handheld console)

The Next Level

With so many people playing video games, it is not surprising that these games have developed so quickly. And they are everywhere — in arcades and on our computers, home consoles, handheld consoles, and mobile devices like phones and tablets.

Video games have become a common part of the world in which we live, and they will continue to evolve as technology develops. Graphics and sound will improve, as will the ways players can interact with games.

The future of video games is very exciting!

Glossary

arcade (*noun*)	a place with coin-operated game machines
Blu-ray (*noun*)	a kind of disc used to store games or movies
broadband internet (*noun*)	high-speed internet access
CD-ROMs (*noun*)	discs that stored and played computer software or games
combat (*noun*)	fighting between different sides
console (*noun*)	an electronic device for playing video games
cosmonaut (*noun*)	a Russian astronaut
electrical engineers (*noun*)	people who design and build electrical devices
evolved (*verb*)	changed over a long period of time
graphics (*noun*)	images on a screen
hardware (*noun*)	machinery or equipment
interact (*verb*)	to respond to a touch or other action
interactive (*adjective*)	able to respond to touches or other actions
interchangeable (*adjective*)	able to be swapped with something else
mimics (*verb*)	imitates or copies
motion-sensitive (*adjective*)	able to sense movement
platform (*noun*)	a raised surface that a person can stand on
role-playing games (*noun*)	games where the player creates a character to play as
ruins (*noun*)	old buildings that are partly destroyed
software (*noun*)	a computer program that has a particular purpose
versions (*noun*)	different forms of something
virtual (*adjective*)	a computer-generated environment that appears and feels real to the user
word processing (*verb*)	using a computer to write documents

Index

arcade games 4, 12–15, 16, 17, 22, 28, 29, 30, 31

augmented reality (AR) 27

Auto Race 20, 28

Bertie the Brain 6, 7, 28

board games 4, 6

Brown Box 11, 28

Cho Chabudai Gaeshi 15, 29

Computer Space 13, 14, 28

consoles 4, 9, 10–11, 16–19, 20–21, 22, 28, 29, 30, 31

Dance Dance Revolution 15, 29

Game Boy 20, 21, 29

graphics 5, 11, 15, 17, 20, 25, 30, 31

handheld console 4, 20–21, 27, 28, 29, 30

hardware 7, 31

home computers 4, 22–24, 30

internet 18, 19, 24, 31

Microvision 20, 28

motion-sensitive gaming 18, 21, 31

MUD1 25, 28

Mystery House 23, 29

Nintendo Switch 21, 29

Nintendo Wii 18

Noughts and Crosses 6–7, 28

Odyssey 11, 28

Pac-Man 17

PlayStation 2 19, 29

Pokémon Go 27, 29

Pong 14, 16, 28

retro games 9

Second Life 25, 29

software 7, 31

Space Invaders 14, 15, 28

Spacewar 8–9, 13, 28

Tennis for Two 7, 28

text-based adventure games 22–23, 24, 25, 28, 29

universities 7, 8, 9, 13

virtual reality (VR) 26, 27

virtual-world game 25

Zork 23, 28

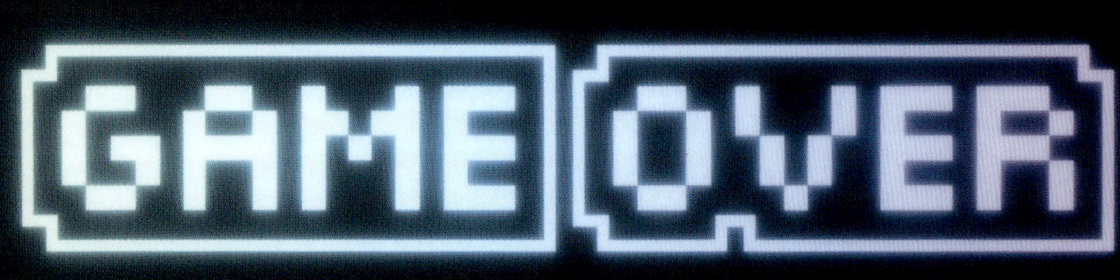